AF454361

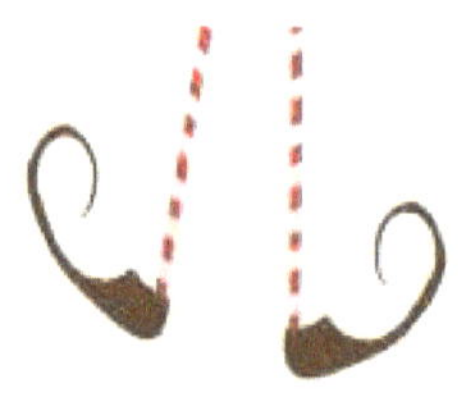

Santa Claus and the Magic Miracle Powder

ISBN: 978-960-9627-05-4

2012 © EVANGELIA STRATI Publishing: BOOKSTAGE

Writer: EVANGELIA STRATI

Cover: BLANK PAGE

Illustration: NIKOLETTA KARIPI

Laughter, laughter and joy

come on children, enjoy!

Merry Christmas

Once upon a time, on exactly twenty days and eight hours before the glorious Christmas night, something so ordinary but also out of the ordinary happened.

The elf - you know, the one with the pointed ears, the thin tail and the rosy cheeks - walked into Santa's workshop pulling a trolley full of letters from the children. He had worked very hard to collect all of them on time.

He emptied the trolley and placed the letters on a big table for Santa to read, so that the next day all the elves would work together to prepare the presents. Surely the fairies would lend them a little hand.

Well, this is the ordinary part.

The out of the ordinary is the expression on Santa's face while he was reading the letters.

Look how he is lifting his eyebrows! How he is twitching his red nose! He seems to be getting angry! How can this be possible?

Santa being angry at the children! This is just not possible!

But wait a minute! You should see this! He starts throwing the letters around. He walks up and down, twirls his moustache and mutters something. There is no doubt that something is very seriously wrong here.

Huff and puff, huff and puff

aw, aw, aw!

I've been struck

by such a great misfortune!

Oh, here comes Mrs. Claus! Now we're sure to find out what has happened since nothing escapes her attention. So let's go closer and listen.

'What's the matter dear? Why are all these letters scattered on the floor?'

'A great misfortune has befallen me. Such a great misfortune!'

'Oh come on now! Stop acting like a child! By the way, aren't these the children's letters on the floor?'

'Yes, they are.'

'Do you want to tell me exactly what these letters are doing on the floor?'

'Oh, but it's such an unbelievable misfortune!'

'Come on dear! Talk to me! You're driving me mad!'

Within seconds Santa starts telling her the story of the great misfortune that struck him.

The letters he got from the children were not what they used to be. Their writing was different; it wasn't the old cheerful and carefree writing. The children were no longer asking for toys and sweets. They were not asking for dolls, toy cars and soldiers. They wanted neither motorbikes nor aeroplanes. No, none of these things were good enough anymore.

'Oh my! What a misfortune indeed!', Mrs. Claus exclaims looking very worried now.

'So what do the children want instead, dear?

'They want something I have not got. So how can I give it to them?'

'You have plenty of time to look for it and find it. It's quite long till the Holly Night. Don't lose heart!'

Mrs. Claus was a very optimistic person and never lost her calm.

'But that's what this misfortune is all about. I cannot find what they are asking me to.'

'Can you not? You? Santa himself? But what on earth are they asking you to bring them?'

'The children are no longer happy. They no longer laugh.'

Mrs. Santa nearly fell off her armchair.

She can't believe the terrible things she's just heard. How this could be possibly happening?

'Well, it is happening though' Santa nodded his head sadly.

'The children have stopped being children and have started to think the way grown-ups do. They are concerned with grown-ups' problems and this is why they have stopped playing and behaving the way they are meant to. Their letters are the clear proof of this. They are asking for things that adults need; a job, money, cars, houses...'

'Oh no! This is so terrible! I'm sure there is an explanation to this. There must be! Shall we go through their letters more carefully to find out what is wrong?'

'We don't need to, my dear. I already know what is wrong and that's why I am so sad.'

'Well, share it with me then. Why have the children stopped being children?'

'It's because grown-ups have stopped laughing. Laughter has disappeared from people's homes and as a result children have learnt to act all serious and adult-like.'

'But, this can't be happening. Children can't lose their laughter.'

'Children have learnt from adults to take things seriously and the magic from their souls is gone. They have stopped believing in miracles!'

Santa Claus
this year I would like to
get me a job for dad and a
stove for my grandmother
Thank you
John

'Oh, magic can't just disappear from the children's souls. Surely this can be fixed.'

'Yes, it can be fixed. But how?'

'I'm sure you can help the children find their lost smile. To believe that miracles happen all the time; every moment, every hour. This wonderful world wouldn't exist without miracles. And who else other than Santa himself is the best person to remind children of this? That's why I'm telling you; don't be sad, you'll think of something.'

The little elf, sat in the corner all this time, had heard everything. How strange all these sounded to him! Children lost their smile! He thought this sounded like a song without its melody.

Then he jumps up and starts shouting.

'But this is not possible! A song without music is not a song.

Music soothes our soul.

It opens up our heart.

A child wants to be charmed

but how can this be done

without a chant?

Santa looks at the elf rather puzzled. He scratches his head, strokes his long beard and suddenly cries out:

'Yes, you're right my little elf! A song without music is not a song!'

'Ho, ho, ho' he cries happily and grabs his lady from the waist and starts dancing with her a wild dance. What a sight! The two of them suddenly dancing and prancing all over the place!

After they danced for a while, Santa summons all his helpers and gives them instructions about the children's presents.

'Listen to me carefully.

This year the presents we'll give to the children will be a bit different.

We'll give everyone a song.

Not an ordinary song but a magic song!

It will contain the magic of miracles, the Magic Miracle Powder!

Quick, get the Miracle potion ready.

The recipe is very simple.

You'll need to put an ounce of ......

two ounces of ....

three ounces of ....

and lastly half an ounce of ....

Stir everything really well and the Miracle potion is ready!'

They all run around happily and get down to work.

The little elf however stays behind and looks confused. Santa notices it and explains to him:

'The song, my little friend, will have the Magic Miracle Powder in it.

The children are the grown-ups' song but grown-ups can't hear it anymore because children have lost their melody, their music; children have lost their laughter.

Well, we are going to give them back their lost music.

So this will be Santa's present; a magic song. That's how the children will be able to believe in miracles again. They will start laughing again.'

The little elf, overwhelmed with happiness, puts his arms around Santa's waist and gives him a hug. It was so lucky he had solved the problem because... we can't have a song without music.

Then they all start to sing the magic song.

Laughter, laughter and joy
come on children, enjoy!

Our soul longs
to hear beautiful songs.
Don't talk like a grown-up
just drink from this cup!

Let the joy of love
fly to your heart like a dove.
Being a child is magic
losing your faith is tragic.

Laughter, laughter and joy
come on children, enjoy!

The following day, on Christmas day, Santa's song could be heard from every house you walked past. The children were singing it!

There was laughter and joy everywhere.

Their laughter was so vivid that it soon spread to adults. They were next to start laughing.

This is how Santa using his Magic Miracle Powder managed to give back to the children their lost innocence, their carefree and delighted laughter, their faith in miracles.

Even adults began to regain their faith in miracles.

Life itself is a great miracle after all, isn't it?

And we all live happily ever after.

With laughter and real joy.

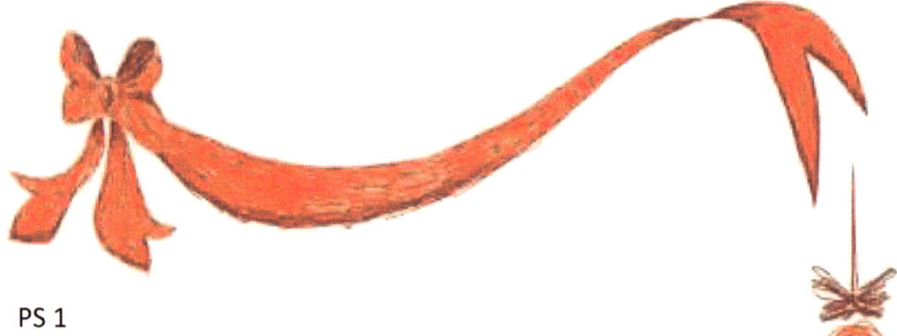

PS 1

Now I'm going to let you in on a secret, but please don't tell anyone. I know the recipe for Santa's Magic Miracle Powder. Honestly I do! One night, while I was sleeping, the little elf came to me and whispered it to my ear. He advised me to share it with good children only. Well, since I know how well-behaved you are, I'll share it with you right now:

RECIPE FOR MAGIC MIRACLE POWDER

an ounce of fairy-laughter powder,

two ounces of elf-joy powder,

three ounces of star-happiness powder

and finally

half ounce of caster naughtiness powder.

Mix them well and the Miracle potion is ready!

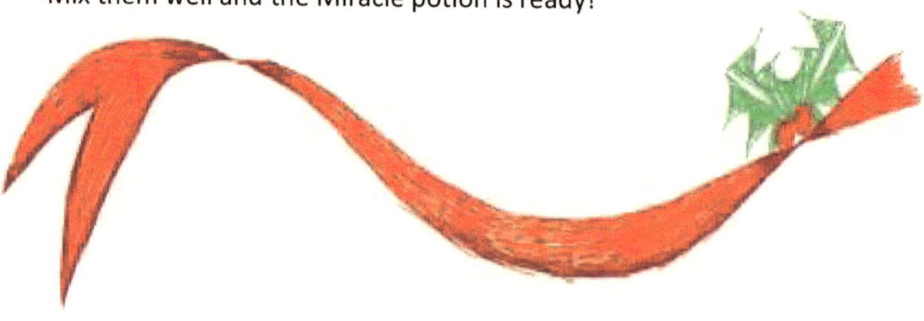

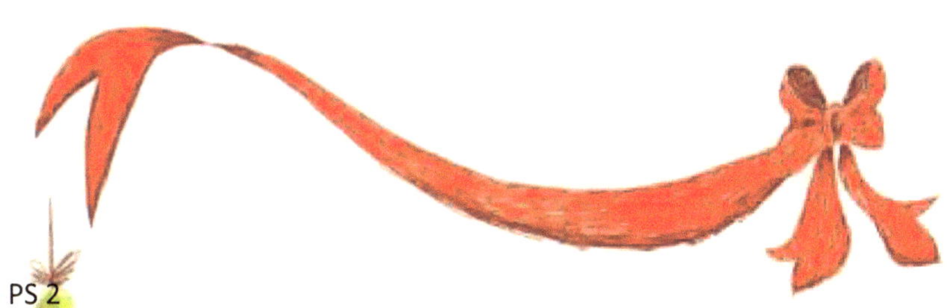

PS 2

I will let you in on another little secret too. I know very well that you try really hard to stay awake waiting for Santa to bring your presents but you never make it. You always fall asleep. Well, I have another secret recipe for a magic drink. You can drink it in the evening and it'll keep you awake. Beware though! The drink stops being magic if you don't believe in miracles.

RECIPE FOR MAGIC DRINK

1 cup of milk

30 grams of milk chocolate

1 teaspoon of honey

a bit of cinnamon

1 teaspoon of chocolate truffle

or

1 tablespoon of whipped cream

or

both chocolate truffle and whipped cream.

INSTRUCTIONS

Heat the milk gently in a saucepan and add the chocolate, the honey and the cinnamon. Stir until the chocolate melts.

Remove the saucepan from the stove and pour the drink in a cup. Sprinkle the chocolate truffle on top or add the whipped cream or use both if you want.

Drink it and wait.

*** Remember! It won't work unless you believe in miracles.

Everything around us is a miracle!

Laughter, laughter and joy

come on children, enjoy!

Merry Christmas

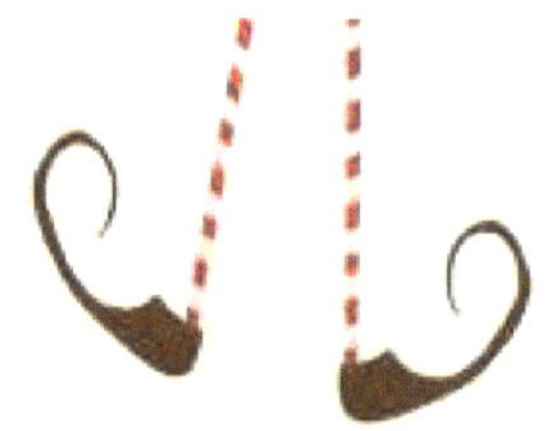

Other books by the author:

- Creative Tales and Magical Treats: Creative writing for kids

- Story Snacks : Writing Magical Recipes for Young Writers

- Larry the Watermelon: A football Star: A Fairy tale & A Workbook of Creative writing for kids

- Rosie and Berry: The competing Cherry Twins: A Fairy tale & A Workbook of Creative writing for kids

- Margery the Strawberry: The true beauty: A Fairy tale & A Workbook of Creative writing for kids

- Emon the Lemon: The road to bravery: A Fairy tale & A Workbook of Creative writing for kids

About me

My name is Evangelia Strati, and I am a passionate writer. I specialize in fairy tales, short stories, and crime novels. I also teach creative writing to children, teenagers, and adults, helping them unlock their creativity and storytelling potential.

I believe that the ability to express oneself freely through writing is essential. While talent plays a role, the willingness to do so is equally important.

Creative writing is excellent for children because it sparks their imagination, enhances their language skills, and boosts self-expression. It helps them explore emotions, solve problems, and build confidence in their ability to communicate ideas and stories.

Through creative writing, children will be introduced to fairy tales, explore their creativity, and learn valuable lessons about important moral values such as kindness and respect, perseverance, teamwork, self-worth, and the importance of cooperation, self-appreciation, and recognizing the strengths in others.